Zen Is Right Now

Zen Is Right Now

*More Teaching Stories and
Anecdotes of Shunryu Suzuki*

Edited by David Chadwick

SHAMBHALA

Shambhala Publications, Inc.
2129 13th Street
Boulder, Colorado 80302
www.shambhala.com

Enso by Shunryu Suzuki
Cover Art: Shutterstock/Exotic Vector/Zenstock
Cover Design: Daniel Urban-Brown
Interior design: Lora Zorian

9 8 7 6 5 4 3 2 1

First Edition
Printed in the United States of America

♾ This edition is printed on acid-free paper that meets the
American National Standards Institute Z39.48 Standard.
♻ Shambhala Publications makes every effort to print on recycled
paper. For more information please visit www.shambhala.com.
Shambhala Publications is distributed worldwide by
Penguin Random House, Inc., and its subsidiaries.

Page 142 constitutes a continuation of the copyright page

Thinking is a good tool—and a bad master.

Alan Watts

Contents

Introduction

Here is a new collection of vignettes about Shunryu Suzuki. The first such publication, *Zen Is Right Here*, was put together a couple of decades ago after the biography of Suzuki, *Crooked Cucumber*, had been out a year. Throughout the ensuing years, I've continued working in this area and have selected some more memories about him that stuck in people's minds and that I thought you, dear reader, might appreciate.

Many of the vignettes herein are from exchanges that happened at Tassajara Zen Mountain Center during *shosan*, a formal question and answer ceremony with Suzuki. In interviews, emails, and conversations, Suzuki's students have related shosan memories . . . more than from any other single source.

Shunryu Suzuki is often referred to as Suzuki Roshi—*roshi* being an honorific meaning "venerable old respected priest." He is best known for the books of his lectures—principally *Zen Mind, Beginner's Mind*, but also *Not Always So* and *Branching Streams Flow in the Darkness*.

In case you don't know anything about Shunryu Suzuki or just need to have your memory refreshed on the basic background, I can do no better than to include some of the introduction from *Zen Is Right Here*. But first, a few words from his students.

Suzuki had a very human style. He never put on airs. He was traditional yet able to take a chance, which he sure did in San Francisco in the sixties—going there and starting Tassajara and all. I've never met anyone like Suzuki since.

Pauline Petchey

I remember he used to say that every teaching of every buddha was really for that moment at that place for those people or that person and that it's imperfect. It's even imperfect at that moment—but it's close to perfect.

Toni (Johansen) McCarty

Instead of putting emphasis on our small mind, on entertaining ourselves with thinking, Suzuki Roshi taught us to "cultivate the big mind."

Jakusho Bill Kwong

Suzuki Roshi told us not to ask questions about our personal problems but to only talk about issues with our practice.

Sue Roberts

I experienced Suzuki Roshi in three ways. There was a kind of worn-out old man, a highly cultured man, and then the Zen master.

Steve Allen

I never saw Suzuki Roshi read from anything when he gave a lecture unless he was looking at a text he was speaking on. He just talked about what was on his mind at the moment, but there was this presence like the sutra come to life.

Bill Lane

Suzuki Roshi was the most remarkable person I ever met. No one else comes close. From Suzuki Roshi I learned that there could be a person like that. Others have mentioned how his movements flowed naturally, and how he sat down or walked. I remember this same quality in his responses to people. He responded very naturally and simply, but from a deep place. Watching him, I could begin to understand what it means to be egoless. He didn't seem to be dragging around heavy feelings the way most of us do, and yet he was bringing his life experience to bear on whatever happened.

Janet Sturgeon

He repeatedly told me that what we've got to do is to establish an American Zen. He's Japanese, and so am I, but he wanted to establish an American Zen, whatever that turned out to be.

Seiyo Tsuji

A Brief Background from the Introduction to Zen Is Right Here

Shunryu Suzuki Roshi, a Soto Zen priest from Japan, arrived in San Francisco in 1959 at the age of fifty-five.

He came to minister to a congregation of Japanese Americans at a temple on Bush Street in Japantown called Sokoji, Soto Zen Mission. *His* mission, however, was more than what his hosts had in mind for him. He brought his dream of introducing to the West the practice of the wisdom and enlightenment of the Buddha, as he had learned it from his teachers. To those who were attracted to the philosophy of Zen, he brought something to do—*zazen* (Zen meditation) and *Zen practice* (the extension of zazen into daily life). A community of students soon formed around him; many of them moved into apartments in the neighborhood so that they could walk to Sokoji for zazen in the early mornings and evenings.

In 1964 a small group of students began to meet for daily zazen in Los Altos, south of San Francisco. Other groups formed in Mill Valley and Berkeley. Suzuki Roshi, as he was called, would join each one once a week, when he could. He lived exclusively at Sokoji until 1967, when Zen Mountain Center was established at Tassajara Springs, deep in the wilderness of Monterey County. This mountain retreat was not only the first Buddhist monastery for Westerners, it also broke from tradition in allowing men and women, married and single, to practice together. It is the setting of many of the accounts in this book. In November of 1969 Suzuki Roshi left Sokoji to found the City Center on Page Street in San Francisco as a residential Zen practice center. He died there in 1971.

To Suzuki Roshi, the heart of a Zen temple is the *zendo*, or zazen hall. There he would join his students in zazen (often just called "sitting"), formal meals, and services in which *sutras*, Buddhist scripture, were chanted. There he would also give lectures, sometimes called *dharma* talks. *Dharma* is a Sanskrit word for Buddhist teaching. Usually one or two forty-minute periods of zazen were held early in the morning and in the evening. Sometimes there would be *sesshin*, when zazen would continue from early morning till night for up to seven days, broken only by brief walking periods, services, meals, lectures, and short breaks. During sesshin Suzuki would conduct formal private interviews with his students, called *dokusan*. We called Suzuki's wife *Okusan*, which is *wife* in Japanese.

Suzuki talked about the paradoxical dual structure of reality—form and emptiness, relative and absolute, then and now. Echoing Dogen, the founder of Soto Zen, he taught that Zen practice is not preparation for something else; that the practice is enlightenment, not something that leads to it. Of course we have to consider the future and plan, but we ground ourselves in the immediate.

Suzuki encouraged his students above all to be themselves and not to use him or Buddhist teaching as a crutch. He said in a lecture, "Your conduct should not be based on just verbal teaching. Your inmost nature will tell you. That is true teaching. What I say is not true teaching. I just give you the hint." He'd say he had no particular teaching. To me, he was just always trying to help us wake up.

Michael Wenger, who has worked a good deal with the Suzuki lecture archive and San Francisco Zen Center publications, once said he had an image of Suzuki with a bow—he was shooting arrows up into the air, hoping they landed on a target. We are all his target. I hope some of the arrows that follow land on you.

David Chadwick
Sanur, Bali, Indonesia
January 6, 2020

Zen Is Right Now

In a shosan ceremony, I walked up toward Suzuki and said, "What now?"

He said, "Don't ask me. Now is now. You have your now. I have my now. That is why now is so important. It is beyond question and answer."

Zen is not something to talk about. It is also something to talk about.

A student said to Suzuki that it seemed to them we need to have some amount of ego and asked, "But how much do we need?"

Suzuki answered, "Just enough so that you don't step in front of a bus."

·

I asked Suzuki Roshi, "When I work in the kitchen, I feel like I'm in the heart of practice. Why do I have to sit so much?"

He answered, "To open your mind wider and wider."

I said, "Inside there's a yes and a no."
  He said, "Follow the yes."

A student said he had disturbing images and thoughts during zazen. Suzuki said, "Whatever bird flies through the sky, the sky doesn't care."

One morning at the end of zazen, Suzuki spoke to the students still facing the wall, repeating an old theme with a new twist: "When you hear the wake-up bell, you should jump out of bed right away. You shouldn't lie there. Otherwise, how can you ever face death, which always comes suddenly? But don't jump out of bed the way I did this morning. I knocked over my kerosene lamp."

Suzuki would frequently hear students complain about others. Often he responded with "Everyone is doing their best."

A student said she did not understand the meaning of her life.

Suzuki answered, "Eternal meaning is in your everyday life. So there is no need to figure out what is the meaning of life."

During a shosan ceremony, I walked up and said, "The stream outside Tassajara has been flowing a long time. I wish to ask it now, how long and how hard must it flow? Listen . . ."

Suzuki Roshi said, "If you notice that point, that is Buddha's sermon."

I first met Suzuki Sensei, as he was called then, at the old Sokoji Temple about a year after he had arrived from Japan. I wanted to know what Zen was. We sat on cushions and he told me about "sitting and doing nothing."

Suzuki said he was most happy when his students shared in the joy of practice. He said that's what Buddhism is— not enlightenment or understanding.

At a celebration dinner following a wedding ceremony, we were sampling a variety of unusual delicacies. Suzuki Roshi picked up something exotic looking and took a big bite. While he was chewing, I asked, "What is that you're eating? I've never seen it before."

Without hesitation, he reached over, deposited the remaining portion in my mouth, and said, "It's delicious. Why don't you try it?" It was lotus root, and it *was* delicious.

A student asked, "Where does the small self come from?"

Suzuki answered, "Actually, there is no small self. We say there is small self, but that is the mistake. We usually make that kind of mistake."

"What is the most important thing for me to do?" I asked Suzuki Sensei. I really wanted to do this practice. I wanted answers.

"Just get up," Suzuki said.

As time passed, my practice matured, and I felt good about it. So I went to Suzuki again. "Now what is the most important thing for me to do?" I asked.

"Just get up," he said.

A student asked, "How is it that big mind can hide so well?"

Suzuki said, "Because it is so big." He paused and then added, "Or because you are too nearsighted."

I couldn't sit in lotus with a straight back. In dokusan with Suzuki, I tried my best but felt awkward. Suzuki said to me, "It's not necessary to hold yourself in any one position."

Suzuki Roshi once said during a sesshin, "Zen is to feel your way along in the dark, not knowing what you will meet, not already knowing what to do. Most of us don't like going so slowly, and we would like to think it is possible to figure everything out ahead of time. But if you go too fast, or are not careful enough, you will bump into things. So just feel your way along in the dark, slowly and carefully."

He gestured with his hand out in front of him, feeling this way and that in the empty air.

"When you do things with this spirit, you don't know what the results will be, but because you carefully feel your way along, the results will be okay. You can trust what will happen."

Sometimes I'm the teacher and you're the student, and sometimes you're the teacher and I'm the student.

One evening in the early sixties, Suzuki started off a lecture by saying, "I've come here to destroy your mind."

Eventually he made it clear he meant the small illusory mind, but it was a chilling statement to many who were present.

One Sunday morning after breakfast, I was in the City Center flop room with other students, reading the Sunday paper. Roshi came in, got a cup of coffee, poured in sugar, drank it, and said, "Strong medicine!" He then did sort of a somersault in his robes, got up, and left.

A student asked what kind of practices Suzuki could advise us to do in order to keep ourselves pure.

He said, "Zazen practice. There is no secret."

What zazen really is has been explained in many different ways. One day Suzuki Roshi put it very simply: "It's just to be ourselves."

Suzuki once described Zen practice as putting a snake in a bamboo tube. He said that within limitations, true joy can be found, "and that is the only way to know the whole universe."

During my first year or so of intense zazen practice, I started having experiences that I thought were unique, unusual, and something to do with attainment of enlightenment. I requested an interview with Roshi and told him of my experiences, expecting praise and recognition.

He just said, "Hmm, soon you won't be having this problem. This is common with beginning students. Your practice is okay, though. Just keep sitting."

A student asked Suzuki, "What is enlightenment?"

"Enlightenment?" Suzuki said. "I think you won't like it."

In a lecture Suzuki said that emptiness will be realized when we are involved in some activity completely, that then we will disappear and that we'll realize that what we thought was "us" is just activity—no one's activity. He said that is nothingness, or emptiness, and it is not somewhere else; it's right here. The proof could be found in practicing zazen.

I remember at Sokoji in the early days, after sitting and chanting the Heart Sutra, how Suzuki Sensei would bow to each of us as we departed. But before he walked to the exit to do that, he would say, "Thank you for your effort."

A student said to Suzuki that she kept trying and trying but just couldn't get anywhere in her zazen, that her legs hurt all the time and she couldn't stop thinking.

"That is our practice," Suzuki said. "Our way is to sit with painful legs and wandering mind."

A student asked, "What do Zen masters do when they're alone together?"

Suzuki said, "They laugh a lot."

I asked Suzuki how to decide which way to go when the path divides.

He answered, "Don't hesitate. Don't think which way is good or bad. When you do not think about it, you will intuitively know which way to go."

I was moved to the core by an insight and decided to check it out with Suzuki Roshi. I asked him if this flash of realization I'd had was an enlightenment experience. When he said yes, I asked if this was what life was like for him all the time. He smiled and said, "Well, it's like when you hear a bird sing."

We were having dokusan on a hot day in August in Suzuki Roshi's office in the city. We were both sitting on the floor, face to face. "What is this bowing?" I asked. Suddenly he got up, came over to my side, and started bowing. Up down, up down, up down. "This is how we do it," he said.

I thought to myself, What is this man doing? Why is he going on bowing for so long?

I have been aware of every bow I have done since then, always with the same question: "What is this bow?"

At one of the lectures, Suzuki told about how he'd been invited to a college class to talk about Zen. He said, "They asked me all kinds of questions, like 'When you talk about reality, do you mean phenomena, or the noumena behind the phenomena?' I didn't know how to answer!" Suzuki laughed and said, "I just had to tell them that is not our way."

In zazen, leave your front door and your back door open. Let thoughts come and go. Just don't serve them tea.

A student asked, "When does my life express the dharma and when does it not?"

Suzuki answered, "Your life always expresses the dharma."

I went to Suzuki Roshi's cabin at Tassajara to ask his advice. He was such a little man, not even five feet tall, but I never thought of him that way. To me, his brightness covered the whole doorway as he invited me in. I told him I was feeling so bad and I didn't know what to do, that I had tried to forget about it in zazen and in my work but that for some reason I was so discouraged and down.

"It will not always be this way," he said. "It may seem so, but things will change."

A student asked Suzuki, "You said we should extend ourselves in practice. In what direction should we extend ourselves?"

Suzuki said, "There is no direction but to be kind to everything, one by one."

Suzuki said that rather than having one or more objects to worship, we focus on whatever it is we're doing at the moment.

Once Suzuki was asked, "How do you know when you're enlightened?"

He responded, "When you no longer complain."

A non-Buddhist may think I am a Buddhist, but I don't think I am a Buddhist. If it is necessary for them to call me something, or to call myself something, maybe, for the sake of convenience, I can be a Buddhist. That's okay. I am happy to be a Buddhist.

At a Zen Center picnic in Golden Gate Park, Suzuki arrived in his robes. A baby blanket on the ground caught his eye. He lay down on it, rolled up in it, and just lay there a while.

A student asked if there was some special reason or meaning when we hit the bells.

Suzuki answered, "To hit the bell means to produce an independent buddha one after another. *Gong!* One independent buddha appears. *Gong!* The next buddha appears and the prior buddha disappears. So, one by one, striking the bells we produce buddhas, one buddha after another. That is our practice."

When I arrived at Bush Street, I had on a bright-orange, large-brimmed, floppy straw hat, purple aviator glasses, enormous hoop earrings, beads with bells, flowers, feathers, and shoes straight out of The *Wizard of Oz*. My sister was similarly attired. We exchanged quizzical glances over the dark and serious atmosphere of the Buddhist church, but when Suzuki Roshi saw us, his face lit up. He gave us instruction in zazen, and we sat together for a few minutes.

Then he looked at us with a grin and said, "When you continue meditation, the more you come to understand life, the more you will see that life is suffering."

We nodded as if we understood and hurried out to the street. We didn't like what he said about suffering, but we knew the smile was genuine. Although I was deep in a fog of confusion, some clarity began to enter my world.

I'd been feeling discouraged and was getting down on myself. Then, in a lecture, my spirits were lifted when I heard Suzuki Roshi say, "There is no difference between our buddha nature and Buddha's buddha nature."

In dokusan I told Suzuki Roshi that zazen was like standing on your head: Standing on your head has no point or goal. It's easy to do but hard to keep doing. He didn't say anything, just nodded a little bit. That evening in his lecture he said, "You know, somebody told me today that zazen is like standing on your head, and this is very true."

Suzuki's wife, Mitsu, wrote:

As he was so single-minded, I tried to think of something to get his attention. "I have a boyfriend," I said one day.

"Bring him over," he replied. "I want to make sure he's right for you."

Suzuki would sometimes use the terms *student* and *disciple* in his lectures. A student asked Suzuki if he was considered a disciple. Suzuki answered, "There are those who are practicing for themselves and those who are practicing for others. Those who are practicing for others are my disciples."

A student who had been getting up well before the wake-up bell and sitting alone asked Suzuki if he could explain what it means to be a serious Zen student.

Suzuki responded, "Don't try to be serious. Just keep up with our practice. Don't try to get up earlier than other people. Stay in bed. Okay?"

A student asked Suzuki what exists.

Suzuki responded, "Nothing exists. We may think something exists, but it's changing moment after moment. That is dharma nature, which goes on and on and on."

Then the student said, "So change exists."

Suzuki answered, "Change, but not something. This is a very funny discussion. It doesn't exist at all!"

Suzuki Roshi indicated, somewhat obliquely, that I should be more in control of myself and my boyfriends. Things had gotten pretty complicated. He said I had to set some limits. "After all," he said, "I feel the same way."

Once, Suzuki was asked what the difference is between sitting zazen on the floor and in a chair. He said, "The only difference is the legs."

Suzuki said in a talk that there's no special way to achieve buddhahood, but that we shouldn't think in terms of "this is buddha and that is not buddha," or "this is zazen and that is not zazen." He said we should study this point more.

A student asked him just how we should study that point.

Suzuki hit the little table in front of him hard with his stick and said fiercely, "Like this!" Then he laughed and said softly, "Do you understand?"

Suzuki Roshi once said in a lecture that we practice Zen so we can appreciate our old age.

Don't kill is a dead precept. *Excuse* me is an actual working precept.

When we first moved into the City Center, the neighborhood was pretty wild. Not long after the move, a student was sweeping the front steps. A teenage girl across the street had put her radio in the second-floor window, pointed out and blasting. She was boogying and hollering out the window to the rhythm of the music. Suzuki Roshi was in the front hall and stepped outside to see what was happening. I was just walking up the steps. The student with the broom shook his head and said to Suzuki Roshi that he couldn't see how to fit this into his practice. Suzuki laughed and roared up at the girl somewhat with the beat, spun around on his heels, and went back into the building.

A student said, "Unless I misunderstood what you said the other night, the motivation to improve is itself ignorance."

Suzuki answered, "Ignorance means, in another word, *concrete*. To be caught by a concrete idea is ignorance."

Whenever Suzuki had to go somewhere, he had to be driven. Whether it was to the dentist, a Japantown newspaper, the home of a member of the Japanese American congregation for a service, or another zendo, something would have to be arranged. It was suggested to Suzuki that he learn to drive so he wouldn't have to be so dependent on others to take him places. He clearly enjoyed doing other things on his own, such as studying or cleaning the temple.

Suzuki responded, "I don't want to drive. I never want to be alone."

During lectures, Suzuki would frequently say, "Do you understand?" A student asked him why he asked that so often.

Suzuki laughed and said, "What I am saying is, 'Do you agree with me?' I'm asking if there is any mistake in my way of thinking."

During a lecture, Suzuki Roshi had talked about desire and its place in our psyche. In the question-and-answer afterward, someone said, "But Roshi, I thought we were supposed to get rid of desire."

He said, "If you had no desire, you'd be dead."

A student said to Suzuki, "I feel pretty foolish. How do you feel?"

Suzuki replied, "Ah. Yeah, I feel the same way."

After I had been practicing for a little over a year, I started meeting with Suzuki Roshi on a regular basis. I brought him many questions about how Zen practice applied to contemporary American life and to my own life, particularly to my work environment. He rarely gave specific advice but rather encouraged continuous practice as the best way to resolve difficulties. During one of our meetings, I described a particularly sensitive situation at work, involving complex personal politics. "What do you think I should do?" I asked.

Ignoring my plea for him to solve my problem, he simply said, "You have to go back to the source of your karma."

Suzuki told us we stuck to naturalness too much, and when we stick to it, that's not natural anymore. He said, "The only true naturalness is when you are you in its true sense in this moment."

A student was crying about how traumatic their early years were at home. Suzuki said, "Every great Zen master had an unhappy childhood."

When I lived on the Iron Range of northern Minnesota, I reached out to connect with my old teacher, whom I missed deeply. I never expected Suzuki to write back. He was not good at returning letters. But he did. I checked the mail one morning and there it was. I recognized the handwriting immediately. How wonderful! It was just a short note, and I don't remember much of what it said. What I remember most is how he ended it. Suzuki was absentminded and forgetful his whole life. At the end of his letter, he wrote, "I may not remember your name, but I will always remember you."

The important thing about zazen is not that it gives you power but that it gives you possibility.

I asked Suzuki if we were still supposed to count our breaths in zazen. I said that sometimes I would count for five minutes and then I'd forget about it or just stop. I asked him then if he'd just tell me what to do—count my breath or not count my breath.

He said, "That is not my problem. It's your zazen, not my zazen."

I took Suzuki and Katagiri to a planetarium in San Francisco one afternoon. Katagiri paid attention, but Suzuki slept through the whole show and had to be awakened when the lights came on. Back on the street, I asked them both how they liked it.

"Very interesting," said Katagiri.

"Wonderful," said Suzuki.

"But you slept through the whole thing!" I said.

We all three looked at each other and burst out laughing at the same moment.

Suzuki said that if we practiced zazen sincerely, we could gradually become free from enslavement to compulsive intellectual and emotional activity. He said calming the intellect would happen first, but that calming emotions was not so easy and would take longer.

A student asked Suzuki, "Where does the mind go when it's not here?"

Suzuki answered, "Mind does not come and go. Mind is always here. The mind that goes wandering about is not true mind."

I told Suzuki Roshi what I was experiencing, and he said that it was an enlightenment experience, that I'd taken good care of myself and now I had to take care of everything. I asked what he meant by that and he picked up a pencil on his table and said, "You have to take care of this." Then he picked up something else and said, "And this." And he kept picking up things and saying that.

To have what Buddha says in your mind is not so good, but to have a mischievous idea in your mind is sometimes very agreeable.

A student said to Suzuki, "If there is no beginning, no end, and no existence, what is the use of a question?"

Suzuki responded, "To recall something that is unknown, to address Buddha."

One day at Sokoji, Suzuki Roshi was up at the altar getting ready to perform a service. He was adjusting some of the many memorial tablets for the Japanese American congregation. Suddenly the whole bunch came down like an avalanche. He turned to face us, smiling happily, and pointed to his head.

A student asked, "How can we help each other?"

Suzuki answered, "The best way to help others is to have good practice. To help others is not different from helping yourself. There is no you and others—it is not two. You see? That is the first principle. Even intellectually, this is the reality we should accept—ultimate reality."

He said to me, "The most important thing for you is to develop patience. So don't fight. That is the key—don't fight."

I realized he meant not only not to fight with others but, even more so, not to fight with myself.

.

A student asked Suzuki, "Isn't the idea people get of being independent a delusion?"

He said, "Yes. Independence is a delusion. We are dependent on everything."

Once when Suzuki was quite sick and being helped to a bed, he said, "Now I can be a little child. I don't have to be a Zen master."

A student asked what the relationship was of one moment to the next moment.

Suzuki said, "One answer is there is no relationship. Another answer is there is a relationship. That is why I'm laughing, you know. If I have to say something, you know, I must say it in two ways."

One evening in a sesshin, all of us sitting there cross-legged, many with aching legs and backs, Suzuki said, "Zazen is hard for you, I know. But remember that zazen is also soft and gentle. Please try to sit with a soft mind like bread dough—you know, how it sticks together and then with fire becomes something wonderful to eat!"

Suzuki was well aware of the strong anti-war sentiment among almost all his students. Earlier in the century he had experienced with dismay the rise of militarism in Japan. He didn't mention it much, but once in a lecture he said:

"Encouraged by trumpets, guns, and war cries, it is quite easy to die. That kind of group practice is not our practice. We practice with people, first of all. But the goal of practice is to practice with mountains and with rivers, with trees and with stones—with everything in the world, in the universe—and to find ourselves in this big cosmos. And in this big world we should intuitively know which way to go."

At the end of sesshin, I felt like I was drifting, spreading out into the air. When it was my turn to ask a question, I couldn't stop laughing. I was terrified. I asked him, "Roshi, I feel like you are going to disappear, like I'm going to disappear, like everything's going to disappear. What should I do?"

He told me, "You don't need to disappear if you don't want to."

In a shosan ceremony, a student approached Suzuki with a determined look and said, "Do you have some question?"

Suzuki said, "Yes, I have a question. Why are you so serious?"

For a moment there was silence. Then the student laughed—and then everybody broke out laughing.

Suzuki said, "If you start to laugh, then it's all right."

Suzuki said once that when he was young, he was interested in Chinese astrology but finally had decided it wasn't necessary to know so much about oneself.

A student asked, "Who is buddha when we bow?"
Suzuki answered, "When you bow, you are the buddha."

One day he invited me into his office to have some tea and asked me what I was doing. I said, "I'm building a subway between San Francisco and Berkeley."

He burst out laughing and said, "That's a long way to go by hammer."

A student asked Suzuki, "What's the difference between you and me?"

Suzuki said, "It's the difference between the little I suffering and the big I suffering."

A student said to Suzuki, "If we don't exercise discrimination, won't we get into situations that are dangerous or bad for us?"

Suzuki answered, "No, I don't think so. I know we feel that way. We feel some need of being smart. But everyone knows what we should do and what we shouldn't. It is not necessary to be so clever, especially in order to understand Buddha's way. One of the difficulties of being a Buddhist is being too smart."

When I first saw Suzuki Roshi, I said, "I've got this problem. I don't understand marriage, sex, and love. I've been married three times. It seems like I could love anybody, or be married to anybody, yet I can't seem to stay married to anybody."

He said, looking shocked, "Even me?!"

Suzuki was asked about the transmission of the teaching. He said that the historical record is not perfect, that there are names and dates that are not accurate, but that historical or scientific information has its limits. He said that what we know is that the spirit has been transmitted through the ages "from warm hand to warm hand."

One day in the late sixties at Tassajara, a student asked Suzuki Roshi, "Why haven't you enlightened me yet?"

His response was quiet and sincere: "I'm making my best effort."

Life is like stepping onto a boat that is about to sail out to sea—and sink.

One afternoon, Roshi compared zazen to a frog sitting on a lily pad waiting for a fly to come. He did a frog imitation, we all laughed, and he said, "The frog doesn't know what will come. He just sits and sees what happens next. Then, whatever happens, he is ready. We should sit like this."

Suzuki and Richard Baker accompanied Trudy Dixon to her family ranch in Montana. When they returned, I picked them up at the airport. As we drove back, Suzuki talked about going horseback riding with Trudy. "I didn't know you knew how to ride horses," I said.

In typical Suzuki fashion, he replied cheerfully, "I don't, but the horse knew how to carry me."

I was in awe of Suzuki Roshi and didn't talk to him until our first dokusan. I wanted to ask about a painful decision I had to make—whether or not to divorce. I tried to hold back tears. As we sat together, I understood that my question held my answer and that he could not answer for me.

After a few minutes, he stood up and walked around me. He sat down again and said, "Your posture is very good."

In that moment, the question formulated: "If I make a difficult decision, and it is wrong, will sitting help me?"

He said, "Yes. Right or wrong, it will help."

Many people had expressed concern about Roshi's health. I asked him, "Roshi, what will we do when you leave us?" My heart was beating so fast, and I could feel the silence in the room. Roshi looked at me with such love and said, "I will never leave you." And he never has.

I asked, "We say, 'Sentient beings are numberless, I take a vow to save them.' What is there to save them from and how do we go about saving them from whatever it is?"

Suzuki answered, "Oh, that's a terrible question to ask!" Students laughed. "Go away! You will get thirty blows!" More laughter. "From what? Why did you come here? Do you know? To know that sentient beings are innumerable is very important. But regardless of the number or difficulty, the answer would be the same. Why should we try to stop war? Anyway, we will not be discouraged in our practice because we have no idea of perfection or attainment. It is something that should be worked toward anyway, or else we won't feel so good."

I would ask, "Do you think I should go to Japan to study and practice? Do you think I should get to know Japanese monastic life?" He would always tell me, "There is no place to go."

At other times I would ask, "Is there something you would like me to do?" He would say, "There is nothing to do. You can do anything you want. Just be yourself." I kept those words in mind, almost like a mantra: "There's no place to go; there's nothing to do."

In a shosan ceremony, a student approached Suzuki and said, "What am I asking you?"

Suzuki answered, "I know what you want to ask me pretty well. But as you don't ask me, I won't answer you."

I asked Suzuki if he would explain the Heart Sutra to me, so I could answer the questions my friends were sure to ask.

"Yes," he said, "but let's do it later. Look at all the sweeping we have to do. Help me with the sweeping first."

We did the sweeping. Then he was off doing something else. It seemed he'd forgotten.

Another day, at breakfast I said to Suzuki, "This would be a good time to tell me about the Heart Sutra, so I can answer my friends' questions."

"Yes, I'll do it, but I need to clean up the dishes first. Okusan is gone, and we have people coming later. So help me clean the kitchen."

We finished up the dishes and then he rushed off.

A student asked why self-centeredness is so hard to overcome.

Suzuki said, "Because you try to get rid of it."

Once at the Oakland Museum, Suzuki Roshi was admiring a *densho*, a hanging bell used in Zen temples. He asked a guard if he could hit it to see what it sounded like but, after some further inquiry, was told he could not. Later, on his way out, he bumped into the bell, as if by accident, and was quite pleased with the sound it made.

In a shosan ceremony, a student walked up, said she had no question, and then asked Suzuki why.

Suzuki answered, "Without any question you are practicing our way. That is true practice. Don't worry about having no question."

Talking about power struggles he'd had with factions of his congregation or in the Soto Zen hierarchy, Suzuki said that when he was young, he had many struggles and that he always won because he'd learned to conquer his impatience. "But now," he said, "I don't feel like that anymore. Now I think it's better to surrender."

We must not forget that we are the center of the universe and are sitting in the center of the universe.

I went to Suzuki and invited him and his wife to go for a sail on the bay in the middle of winter.

"I'll ask Okusan," he said. "Call me Friday and I'll tell you what she says."

On Friday, Roshi said, "I asked Okusan, but I'm sorry, she got sick."

"Oh, that's too bad. What's the trouble?"

"I don't know; maybe it's seasickness."

An awkward polite silence. Then, "Well, maybe you can come without her?"

"I can't," said Roshi quickly. "I have to stay home and take care of her."

A student asked Suzuki if they could practice Buddha's way without knowing Buddha's way intellectually. Suzuki answered that if you could do that, you were very lucky, but that, unfortunately, we cannot practice without intellectual understanding.

The student then asked if they should include the concepts and ideas from their study in their zazen practice.

Suzuki said, "No. At that time we forget."

Suzuki Roshi said that it may not be difficult to be enlightened, but it is difficult not to be attached to it.

In the summer of 1968, an entourage of Japanese and Western Zen teachers visited Tassajara for a couple of days. At a general meeting in the zendo, students were encouraged to ask questions.

Out of the sixty or seventy people in the zendo, I was the only one to raise a hand. I asked, "What is the best way to establish Zen in America?"

It was announced that four of them would answer this question. In dramatic fashion, the first three responses urged us to practice zazen with great determination, to attain enlightenment, and to establish meditation centers throughout the United States.

As the host, Suzuki Roshi was the last to speak. When his turn came, he stood up, quietly said, "I have nothing to say," and walked out a side door.

The zendo literally shook with our laughter as the session came to a surprisingly abrupt end.

A student asked, "Where is our intuition?"

Suzuki answered, "If you know where it is, that is not intuition."

Someone had asked Suzuki why they were so unhappy, and he told them it was because they were so selfish. But then he softened the blow by saying that if we resign from living for our own mundane happiness and "practice our way," we can find lasting joy and composure even in adversity.

In a lecture Suzuki Roshi said, "The Buddha's zazen is a huge umbrella. In India, it is hot, and people need an umbrella to protect them from the sun." He opened an imaginary umbrella, extending his right hand high above his head. "If you want, you can come inside and sit underneath it here with me. As more people come inside, it gets bigger and bigger. It is actually so!"

A student asked Suzuki what to do about getting sleepy in zazen.

Suzuki answered, "That's the worst enemy! The only thing that may help is to get good sleep. And to have good sleep, it is necessary to organize your life. If you have good zazen, it means you have a well-organized life."

With various scales in our mind, we experience things. Still, the things themselves have no scale.

A student asked, "How do I respond with my everyday mind when my house is on fire?"

Suzuki answered, laughing, "On fire? Why don't you get out of it? You will find a good new one."

A student asked what the point was of all this hard practice.

Suzuki said, "So you can die well."

In one shosan, I went up to bow and ask my question, and I couldn't get a clear take on him. He seemed to be becoming a woman, my grandmother, himself—it was all getting mixed up. So my question that arose at that time was "Who are you?"

He said, "Who are you asking?" and I said, "All of you," and he said he was just someone who's saying something, someone with form and color who originally had no form and color, but that basically I was now talking with someone with a body and mind.

I said, "Thank you."

Suzuki Roshi would teach us in various ways not to get too attached to our habits, thoughts, beliefs, and also to our Zen practice. Along those lines he'd say, "Don't stick to an idea." And then he picked up a phrase he'd heard us use and started saying, "Don't go on any trips."

At one of his talks in Los Altos, a woman asked what it was like to sit zazen for so many years.

Suzuki responded, "It's like climbing a mountain—the higher you go the more beautiful the view is—but it gets lonely."

Shortly before Roshi died, I had an interview with him, as I was thinking about becoming more of a full-time sitter and less of an artist. I showed him some small paintings that I had done.

"Hmm," he said. "I think you are really an artist. Paint more, sit less."

A student asked Suzuki, "What are you doing here?" Suzuki answered, "Nothing special."

When Suzuki came back from Japan in 1970, he talked about various things. He was disappointed that he couldn't find an appropriate temple or monastery where his students could practice and get a taste of Japanese Zen and culture. He also expressed dismay in what he saw as degradation of the environment. He knew some of us were concerned about pollution and threats to the environment, but I'd never heard him express concern to that degree before.

And then one day I heard him say, "But you know, if the whole world is destroyed, nothing has happened."

Suzuki said that if we don't have a goal in our practice, we will feel lost, but if we do have a goal, we will actually be lost. So rather than have a goal, he taught us to live with a vow to continue our practice forever.

Hoitsu Suzuki visited his dying father. He was Shunryu Suzuki's eldest son and now abbot of his temple in Japan. Hoitsu was overwhelmed with the size and devotion of Suzuki's following.

Hoitsu said, "I told him, 'You're really fortunate, aren't you, to have all these people care for you.'

"My father answered, 'Yes. It makes me feel happy.' There are many priests who don't find such happiness."

A terminally ill Suzuki concluded the last lecture he gave by saying, interspersed with a few soft laughs, "We don't know how long it takes for us to make the buddha trip. We have many trips: work trips, space trips, various trips we must have. The buddha trip is a very, very long trip. That is Buddhism."

ON THE FIRST SESSHIN...

In the memory of the Buddha's
Nirvana Day, we have Sesshin in
the Sokoji Meditation Hall.

I did not expect to have Sesshin
so soon. It is not one year yet
since I came here. I am very
grateful to the Zen students who
will attend this Sesshin. This
Sesshin will be called The First
Sesshin of Sokoji.

It is very difficult to keep
continuous effort for us, but we
must continue it for ever.

May Shojin Prajna Paramita be
always with us by the mercy of
the Buddha.

Rev. Sunryu Suzuki
Sokoji Temple
San Francisco

February 21, 1960

Each participant in the first sesshin received this remembrance.
The seal of Sokoji is on the left.

The kanji for sesshin from the original cover is on the first page of
this book.

Acknowledgments

Many thanks to those who looked at all the vignettes being considered for this book and helped me decide which ones to use—coconspirator and chief adviser Michael Katz, Cuke Archives associate Peter Ford and his friend Steve Ferguson, Cuke Press cofounder and postmaster Lawrence Burns, keen-eyed Carol Williams, old friend Gregory Johnson, my beloved wife, Katrinka McKay, eldest fine son, Kelly Chadwick. And thanks to Clare Hollander, Secretary of Cuke Archives, for helping in many ways.

Many thanks to Nikko Odiseos, president of Shambhala Publications, for sending me a note in 2019 informing me that *Zen Is Right Here* was published as a Pocket Library edition, commenting that it's one of his favorite books, and for immediately setting this project in motion when I responded that I could do a sequel.

Many thanks to Shambhala editors Matt Zepelin and Samantha Ripley for the time and care they put into this project. Thanks also to Lora Zorian for the book's interior design, Tori Henson and Michael Henton for marketing and publicity support, and Emily Wichland for such attentive copyediting.

Many thanks to all the good people who shared these memories.

And many thanks to Shunryu Suzuki for coming to America.

Further Reading

Anderson, Reb. *Warm Smiles from Cold Mountains: Dharma Talks on Zen Meditation*. Berkeley, CA: Rodmell Press, 1999.

Brown, Edward Espe. *Tomato Blessings and Radish Teachings: Recipes and Reflections*. New York: Riverhead Books, 1997.

Burkett, Tim. *Nothing Holy about It: The Zen of Being Just Who You Are*. Boston: Shambhala Publications, 2015.

Chadwick, David. *Crooked Cucumber: The Life and Zen Teaching of Shunryu Suzuki*. New York: Broadway Books, 1999.

———. shunryusuzuki.com. The Shunryu Suzuki archive with lectures, audio, video, photos.

———. *Thank You and OK! An American Zen Failure in Japan*. Boston: Shambhala Publications, 2007. First published 1994 by Penguin (New York).

———. www.cuke.com. An archival website on Shunryu Suzuki and those who knew him.

———. *Zen Is Right Here: Teaching Stories and Anecdotes of Shunryu Suzuki*. Boston: Shambhala Publications, 2007. Shambhala Pocket Library edition with subtitle The *Wisdom of Shunryu Suzuki*. Boulder, CO: Shambhala Publications, 2019. First published 2001 as *To Shine One Corner of the World* by Broadway Books (New York).

Dogen, Eihei. *Dogen's Genjo Koan: Three Commentaries*. Berkeley, CA: Counterpoint, 2013.

Fields, Rick. *How the Swans Came to the Lake: A Narrative History of Buddhism in America*. Boston: Shambhala Publications, 1992.

Kaye, Les. *Zen at Work: A Zen Teacher's 30-Year Journey in Corporate America*. New York: Three Rivers Press, 1997.

Kwong, Jakusho. *No Beginning, No End: The Intimate Heart of Zen*. Boston: Shambhala Publications, 2010.

McDonald, Marilyn. *A Brief History of Tassajara: From Native American Sweat Lodges to Pioneering Zen Monastery*. San Rafael, CA: Cuke Press, 2018.

Mitchell, Elsie. *Sun Buddhas, Moon Buddhas: A Zen Quest*. New York: Weatherhill, 1973.

Mountain, Marian. *The Zen Environment: The Impact of Zen Meditation*. New York: William Morrow, 1982.

Richmond, Lewis. *Work as a Spiritual Practice: A Practical Buddhist Approach to Inner Growth and Satisfaction on the Job*. New York: Harmony, 2011. First published 1999 by Broadway Books (New York).

Schneider, David. *Street Zen: The Life and Work of Issan Dorsey*. Boulder, CO: Shambhala Publications, 2020.

Storlie, Erik Fraser. *Nothing on My Mind: Berkeley, LSD, Two Zen Masters, and a Life on the Dharma Trail*. Boston: Shambhala Publications, 1997.

Suzuki, Mitsu. *Temple Dusk: Zen Haiku*. Berkeley, CA: Parallax Press, 1992.

Suzuki, Shunryu. *Branching Streams Flow in the Darkness: Zen Talks on the "Sandokai."* Berkeley, CA: University of California Press, 1999.

———. *Not Always So: Practicing the True Spirit of Zen*. San Francisco: HarperOne, 2009.

———. *Zen Mind, Beginner's Mind*. 50th ann. ed. With an afterword by David Chadwick. Boulder, CO: Shambhala Publications, 2020. First published 1970 by Weatherhill (Trumble, CT).

Tipton, Steven M. *Getting Saved from the Sixties*. Berkeley, CA: University of California Press, 1982.

Wenger, Michael. *49 Fingers: A Collection of Modern American Koans*. San Francisco: Dragons Leap Press, 2011.

———. *Wind Bell: Teachings from the San Francisco Zen Center 1968–2001*. Berkeley, CA: North Atlantic Books, 2001.

For additional reading on Shunryu Suzuki, please also see: suzukiroshi.sfzc.org.

Credits

The people listed below are the sources of the accounts in this book, and may or may not be the persons involved in the anecdotes. Credits are organized by page number. The introduction has more information on the venues. More on Shunryu Suzuki, his students, and this book can be found on the website devoted to this work: www.cuke .com.

The image on page 38 is from Shunryu Suzuki's old, worn-out datebook, drawn while he was flying to the United States for the first time in May of 1959.

1: David Chadwick, Tassajara, 1967. 2: Jerry Fuller, Tassajara, 1969. 3: Dennis Samson, Tassajara, 1969. 4: Katharine

Cook, Tassajara, 1967. 5: Katharine Thanas, Tassajara, 1968. 6: Tim Burkett, Tassajara, 1967. 7: Margaret Kress, Tassajara, 1971. 8: David Chadwick, 1968. 9: Pat Herreshoff, Tassajara, 1968. 10: Jack Elias, Tassajara, 1968. 11: Bill Kwong, Sokoji, 1960. 12: Niels Holm. 13: Les Kaye, Los Altos, circa 1965. 14: Tim Aston, Tassajara, 1969. 15: Tim Burkett, Los Altos, circa 1964.

16: Mike Daft, 1968. 17: Sterling Bunnell, Sokoji, circa 1968. 18: Edward Brown, Sokoji, circa 1966. 19: Frances Thompson, Tassajara, 1968. 20: Silas Hoadley, Sokoji, circa 1964. 21: Barrie Mason, City Center, circa 1970. 22: Alan Marlowe, Tassajara, 1969. 23: Bill Kwong, Sokoji, circa 1963. 24: Tommy Dorsey, Tassajara, circa 1971. 25: Peter DiGesu, Sokoji, circa 1966. 26: Elizabeth Tuomi, Tassajara, 1971. 27: Mark Lewis, Tassajara, 1969. 28: Gordon Geist, Sokoji, 1964. 29: Nelda Foresta, Tassajara, 1967. 30: Jeannie Campbell, Sokoji, circa 1966.

31: Daya (Dianne) Goldschlag, City Center, 1971. 32: Paul Shippee, Tassajara, circa 1968. 33: Teah Strozer, City Center, 1971. 34: Chris Miller, City Center, circa 1970. 35: Toni (Johansen) McCarty, Los Altos, circa 1965. 36: Katharine Thanas, Tassajara, 1968. 37: Anonymous, Tassajara, circa 1970. 39: Jane (Westberg)

Schneider, Tassajara, 1969. 40: Marian (Derby) Wisberg, Los Altos, circa 1965. 41: Bill Smith, Tassajara, 1967. 42: Henry Schaeffer, City Center, 1971. 43:Stephen Gaskin, San Francisco, 1969. 44: Bonnie (Slater) Hurst, Tassajara, 1970. 45: Jill Schireson, Sokoji, circa 1967.

46: Anonymous, Tassajara, 1968. 47: Jim Morton, Tassajara, 1967. 48: Mitsu Suzuki, Sokoji, circa 1966. 49: Reb Anderson, Sokoji, circa 1969. 50: Pat Lang, Sokoji, 1969. 51: Blanche Hartman, City Center, circa 1970. 52: Janet Sturgeon, Tassajara, 1970. 53: Pauline Petchey, Sokoji, circa 1963. 54: Bob Halpern, Sokoji, 1969. 55: Lewis Richmond, Tassajara, 1971. 56: David Chadwick, Tassajara, 1970. 57: Elizabeth Sawyer, City Center, 1969. 58: Craig Boyan, Tassajara, 1969. 59: Richard Baker, Sokoji, circa 1965. 60: Harriet Hiestand, Tassajara, 1968.

61: Janet Sturgeon, Tassajara, 1970. 62: Claude Dalenberg, Tassajara, 1968. 63: Les Kaye, Tassajara, Los Altos, 1967. 64: Tony Johansen, Los Altos, circa 1965. 65: David Chadwick, Sokoji, 1966. 66: Tim Burkett, Minnesota, circa 1970. 67: Erik Storlie, Sokoji, 1967. 68: Craig Boyan, Tassajara, 1969. 69: Irene Horowitz, San Francisco, circa 1967. 70: Fred Stoeber, Sokoji, 1966. 71: Paul Alexander, Tassajara, 1967. 72: Bob Walter, City Center, 1970. 73: Peg Anderson,

Los Altos, 1966. 74: Loring Palmer, Tassajara, 1967. 75: Stanley White, Sokoji, 1965.

76: Bonnie Miller, Tassajara, 1971. 77: David Chadwick, City Center, 1970. 78: Silas Hoadley, Tassajara, 1970. 79: Richard Levine, City Center, 1971. 80: Margret Crowley, Tassajara, 1969. 81: Erik Storlie, Tassajara, 1967. 82: Tim Ford, City Center, 1971. 83: Liz Wolf, Tassajara, circa 1968. 84: Peter Schneider, Tassajara, 1967. 85: David Chadwick, Sokoji, 1966. 86: Mary Quagliata, Tassajara, 1967. 87: Larry Hansen, Sokoji, 1969. 88: Dennis Samson, Mill Valley, 1970. 89: Molly Jones, Tassajara, 1969. 90: Sue Satermo, City Center, 1970.

91: Beverly Horowitz, Sokoji, 1965. 92: Edward Brown, Tassajara, circa 1969. 93: Mel Weitsman, Sokoji, circa 1964. 94: Frank Anderton, Tassajara, 1968. 95: Tim Burkett, San Francisco, 1969. 96: Dot Kostriken, Tassajara, 1967. 97: Liz Wolf, Tassajara, 1968. 98: David Chadwick, Tassajara, 1969. 99: Richard Baker, Sokoji, 1963. 100: Anonymous, Tassajara, 1969. 101: Tim Burkett, Los Altos, 1964. 102: Cheryl (Loskutoff) Faus, Tassajara, 1967. 103: Lanier Graham, Oakland, 1970. 104: Sally Block, Tassajara, 1968. 105: Peter Schneider, Sokoji, 1969.

106: Edward Brown, Tassajara, 1968. 107: Durand

Kiefer, Sokoji, 1965. 108: Reuven Benyuhmin, Tassajara, 1970. 109: Jonathan Altman, Tassajara, circa 1968. 110: Les Kaye, Tassajara, 1968. 111: Doug Bradle, Tassajara, 1969. 112: David Chadwick, Tassajara, 1968. 113: Erik Storlie, Tassajara, 1967. 114: Jeanne DiPrima, Tassajara, 1971. 115: Tim Burkett, Los Altos, circa 1965. 116: Evelyn Pepper, Tassajara, 1968. 117: Tim Buckley, Sokoji, 1966. 118: Katharine Thanas, Tassajara, 1968. 119: Peter DiGesu, Tassajara, 1970. 120: Bill Smith, circa 1965.

121: Peter DiGesu, City Center, 1971. 122: Alan Rappaport, Tassajara, 1968. 123: David Chadwick, City Center, 1970. 124: Jerome Peterson, Sokoji, circa 1965. 125: Hoitsu Suzuki, City Center, 1971. 126: David Chadwick, City Center, 1971. 127: Sesshin remembrance—from Betty Warren.

Resources

The following resources are available at cuke.com/zirn:

Outtakes from this book and its companion volume,
   Zen Is Right Here

An expanded bibliography

Materials exclusive to the site, such as *Chronicles of Haiku Zendo*,
   edited by Barbara Hiestand (Los Altos, CA: Haiku Zendo
   Foundation, 1973), *Wind Bell* (publication of the San
   Francisco Zen Center), 1961–1998, and *Remembering the
   Dragon: Recollections of Suzuki Roshi by his Students*, edited by
   Gil Fronsdal (San Francisco Zen Center, 2004)

Links to the massive cuke.com history of Shunryu Suzuki
   and those whose lives touched his—and whatever
   else comes to mind

Library of Congress Cataloging-in-Publication Data

Names: Chadwick, David, 1945– editor.
Title: Zen is right now: more teaching stories and anecdotes of
Shunryu Suzuki / Shunryu Suzuki; edited by David Chadwick.
Description: First edition. | Boulder, Colorado: Shambhala, [2021]
Identifiers: LCCN 2020035831 | ISBN 9781611809145 (hardback)
Subjects: LCSH: Suzuki, Shunryū, 1904–1971—Quotations. |
Spiritual life—Zen Buddhism—Quotations, maxims, etc.
Classification: LCC BQ988.U9 Z47 2021 |
DDC 294.3/927092—dc23
LC record available at https://lccn.loc.gov/2020035831